GW00367658

Other titles in the series:
The Crazy World of Cats (Bill Stott)
The Crazy World of Gardening (Bill Stott)
The Crazy World of Golf (Mike Scott)
The Crazy World of the Greens (Barry Knowles)
The Crazy World of the Handyman (Roland Fiddy)
The Crazy World of Hospitals (Bill Stott)
The Crazy World of Housework (Bill Stott)
The Crazy World of Marriage (Bill Stott)
The Crazy World of Rugby (Bill Stott)
The Crazy World of Sailing (Peter Rigby)
The Crazy World of Sex (David Pye)

This paperback edition published simultaneously in 1992 by Exley
Publications Ltd. in Great Britain, and Exley Giftbooks in the USA.
First hardback edition published in Great Britain in 1990 by Exley
Publications Ltd.

ISBN 1-85015-354-X

A copy of the CIP data is available from the
British Library on request.

Printed in Spain by Grafo S.A., Bilbao.

Exley Publications Ltd, 16 Chalk Hill, Watford, Herts WD1 4BN,
United Kingdom.
Exley Giftbooks, 359 East Main Street, Suite 3D, Mount Kisco,
NY 10549, USA.

the CRAZY world of CRICKET

Cartoons by
Bill Stott

EXLEY

MT. KISCO, NEW YORK • WATFORD, UK

"*You're a new member aren't you? … Played much?*"

"I don't think their bowling is up to much ..."

*"It doesn't do anything for team morale,
the bowler wearing a helmet ..."*

"My mother bought it for me when I was at school in the mistaken belief that I'd grow into it."

"You know what funds are like – that is the new ball!"

"It's very kind of you darling, but I don't know what the team will think of it."

"O.K. – now try slanting it across him – pitch it on middle and off, but he's not good off his legs. Failing that, knock his head off."

"Perfect whites, brilliant average, pays his subs two seasons in advance … he makes me sick."

"The vicar hates giving LBW decisions …"

"I see we lost the toss …"

"He's our strike bowler …"

"Your flies are open, son …"

"O.K. men – let's keep it tight, take our chances and give 'em hell. You as well Mervyn …"

"*You don't often see umpires coming to nets …*"

"Relax – the lightning hit the stumps before the ball did."

"Go on – one more over – and you can have my cream cake at tea-time ..."

"Just one of captaincy's hidden hazards ..."

"*Guess whose girlfriend is watching …*"

"Our scorer's obviously been cheating again ..."

"*Phew! Did you have the onions at tea?*"

"The windscreen he just smashed was yours umpire ..."

"Actually, he doesn't get many wickets –
but, boy, can he polish a ball!"

"Well, I thought it was rather harsh. Anyone can lose the toss …"

"We may be in trouble …
the chap counting on his fingers – their scorer."

"I thought it was the bowler who got the congratulation for an LBW decision – not the umpire!"

"He's gone from fast to fast-medium, medium to slow-medium, to slow, and nowadays sometimes doesn't make it to the crease!"

"He obviously doesn't rate the bowling …"

"He's a mine of information – he'll tell you the difference between a googly, chinaman, knuckle ball, in-swinger, out-swinger, but he can't bowl any of them."

"This bowler's got me foxed. I can't decide whether to concentrate on the odd leg glance when his line strays or to blast him all around the ground ..."

"Shame about the rain – I felt full of runs today …"

"Nothing personal Arnold, but could you go to short third man?"

"He's a golfer's cricketer. That one's for singles. That one's a sweeper. That one's for fours. The heavy one's for sixes …"

1

2

"Oh, hard luck! – Caught by a fielder in borrowed trousers!"

"He likes to give it a little air ..."

"Rule No. 428(b): Beware the bowler with the silly action ..."

"… he's probably got your number …"

"Message from the bowler. Do you have any medical insurance?"

"Come on! It wasn't __that__ wide!"

"Can't bowl, can't bat, can't field, but he can certainly shove a sight-screen."

"I don't care if it is his fortieth birthday – he doesn't get another turn."

"*Not out. And please confine removals to the bails only please.*"

"Young Bradshaw's on form today, Vicar?"

"New bat? Buy a new bat? Nonsense – this is just broken in."

*"Nothing to worry about – very erratic –
just the odd straight, fast one …"*

"Oooh look, a magpie – that's unlucky …"

"Who's been buying the scorers drinks?"

1   *"Six pads?"*

2   *"Yes – I've seen this bowler before …"*

1

2 *"It's still yours …!"*

"Oh dearie me! LBW __and__ stepped on wicket!"

"We'll be O.K. here. This bowler hasn't hit a length yet!"

"It happens sometimes at the beginning of the season –
he gets the games mixed up ..."

"We'll find it in a minute – the chewing will raise the seam beautifully."

"*There is absolutely no need for that sort of excess young man.*"

"He never agrees with the captain's declarations."

"Do you want me to stay at long on?"

"That's one six and a Volvo headlamp unit."

"I know I brought you on to buy a wicket, but a no-balled wide plus three from an overthrow is too expensive ..."

"Yoo-hoo darling – Drusilla's waving at you …"

*"Skipper says we can do without the scorers' opinion
thank you very much ..."*

"*I see someone who has had to wash his own whites!*"

"Next season the league's adopting a limited over system for teams of limited ability. Ours is getting three per innings."

"I think he said 'Who turned the shower down?'"

"*Captain! I'd like to point out that, not content with putting three easy chances down, he's pinched my cream cake!*"

"Going by the score, you lot should have made the tea …"

"I see Terry's still smarting over the LBW decision …"

"That's his 'Is it worth it?' look – didn't bowl, dropped three catches and was run out for nought by his best friend."

"And that's the glass eye your grandpapa wrested from the umpire after thirty-nine LBW shouts had been turned down back in 1927."

1

2

P.T.O.

3

4

Books in the "Crazy World" series
($4.99 £2.99 paperback)

The Crazy World of Cats (Bill Stott)
The Crazy World of Cricket (Bill Stott)
The Crazy World of Gardening (Bill Stott)
The Crazy World of Golf (Mike Scott)
The Crazy World of the Greens (Barry Knowles)
The Crazy World of the Handyman (Roland Fiddy)
The Crazy World of Hospitals (Bill Stott)
The Crazy World of Housework (Bill Stott)
The Crazy World of Marriage (Bill Stott)
The Crazy World of Rugby (Bill Stott)
The Crazy World of Sailing (Peter Rigby)
The Crazy World of Sex (David Pye)

The Mini Joke Book series
($6.99 £3.99 hardback)

These attractive 64 page mini joke books are illustrated
in colour throughout by Bill Stott.

A Binge of Diet Jokes
A Bouquet of Wedding Jokes
A Feast of After Dinner Jokes
A Portfolio of Business Jokes
A Round of Golf Jokes
A Romp of Naughty Jokes
A Spread of Over-40s Jokes

The "Fanatics" series ($4.99 £2.99 paperback)

The **Fanatic's Guides** are perfect presents for everyone
with a hobby that has got out of hand. Eighty pages of
hilarious black and white cartoons by Roland Fiddy

The Fanatic's Guide to the Bed
The Fanatic's Guide to Cats
The Fanatic's Guide to Computers
The Fanatic's Guide to Dads
The Fanatic's Guide to Diets
The Fanatic's Guide to Dogs
The Fanatic's Guide to Husbands
The Fanatic's Guide to Money
The Fanatic's Guide to Sex
The Fanatic's Guide to Skiing

Great Britain: Order these super books from your local
bookseller or from Exley Publications Ltd, 16 Chalk
Hill, Watford, Herts WD1 4BN. (Please send £1.25 to
cover postage and packing on 1 book, £2.50 on 2 or
more books.)